I0755004

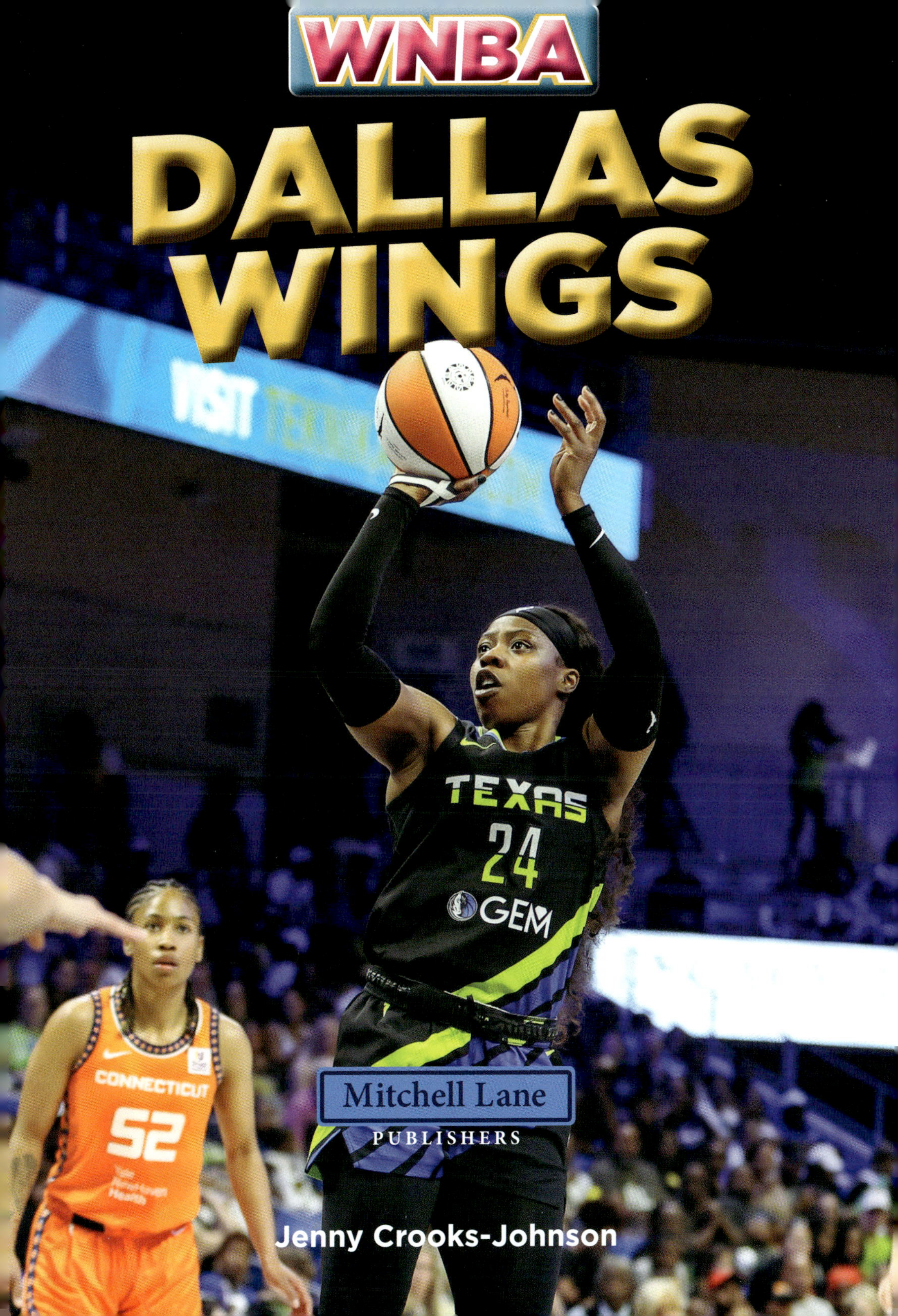
WNBA
DALLAS WINGS
VISIT
TEXAS
24
GEM
CONNECTICUT
52
Mitchell Lane
PUBLISHERS
Jenny Crooks-Johnson

Mitchell Lane
PUBLISHERS

mitchelllanepub.com

2001 SW 31st Avenue
Hallandale, FL 33009

First Edition, 2026.
Author: Jenny Crooks-Johnson
Designer: Ed Morgan
Editor: Tammy Gagne

Series: WNBA
Title: Dallas Wings

Library bound ISBN: 979-8-89260-478-9
eBook ISBN: 979-8-89260-494-9

Photo credits: p. 11, 17, 23 wikimedia; balance Alamy

CONTENTS

Chapter ONE

A BIG WIN FOR THE WINGS

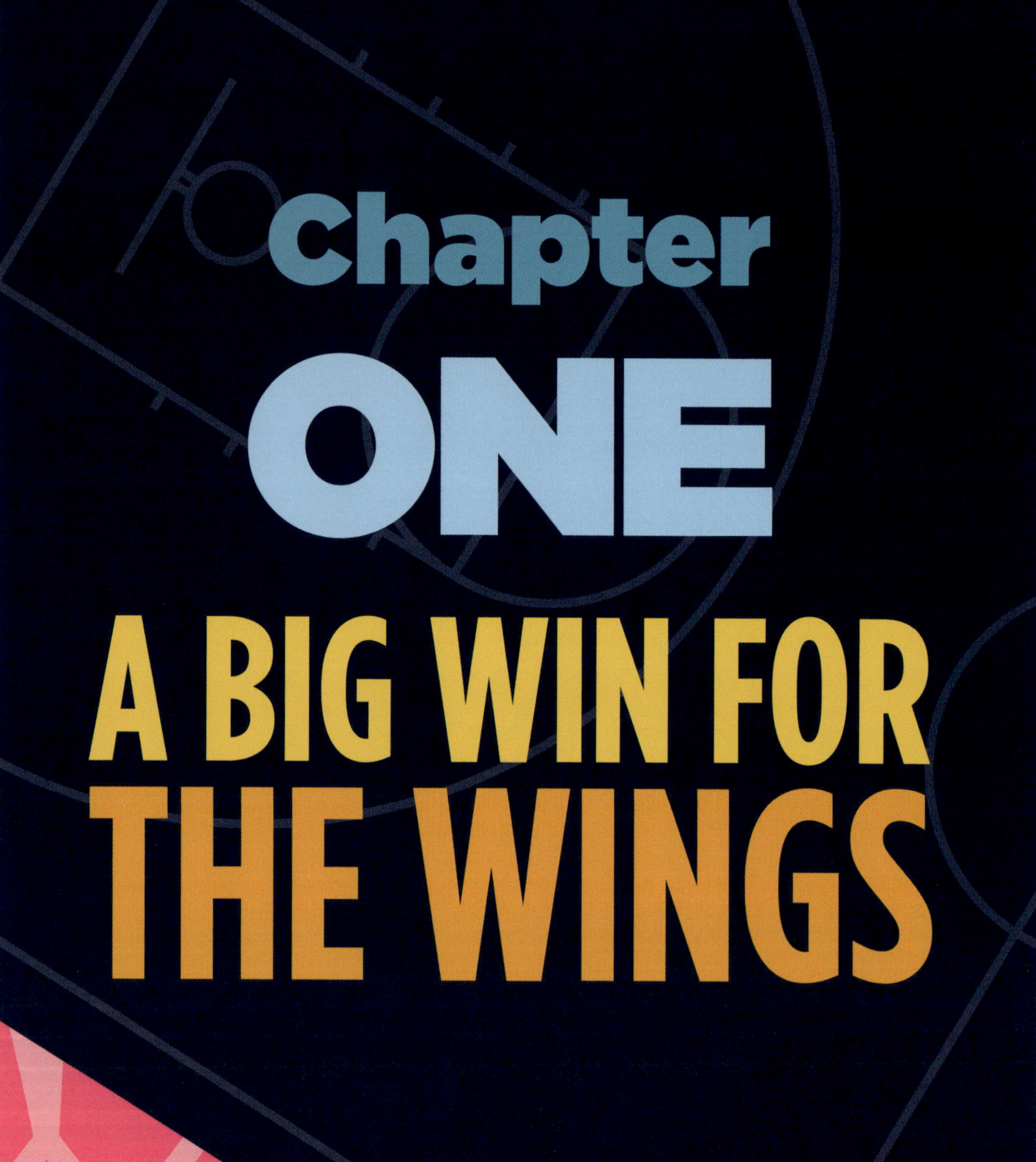

On September 19, 2023, Dallas Wings fans poured into College Park Center in Arlington, Texas. They were there to watch the Wings in the Women's National Basketball Association (WNBA) playoffs. This was the second game in the first round against the Atlanta Dream.

CHAPTER ONE

The first game had been a nail-biter, with the teams trading the lead several times. But the Wings had pulled ahead when it counted most and won with a final score of 94–82. Now the pressure was even higher. They needed to win one more game against the Dream to advance.

The first quarter ended with the Wings down by a single point. Then, about halfway through the second quarter, Awak Kuier made a three-pointer that drove the Wings into the lead. Next, Satou Sabally made a **fast break layup**. Her 2 points extended their lead.

A Big Win for the Wings

FAST FACT

Awak Kuier stands 6 feet, 6 inches (2 m) tall. In June 2022, she became the eighth WNBA player to dunk a ball during a game.

CHAPTER ONE

Arike Ogunbowale was ready to do her part as well, but two Dream defenders stood firmly between this Wings player and the basket. Ogunbowale jumped above them and made her own three-point shot. The crowd went wild. The Wings were now ahead by 7 points. They never stepped off the gas pedal after that. By the beginning of the fourth quarter, Dallas was ahead by more than 20 points.

The Wings won the game 101–74 and moved to the semifinals for the first time since the team moved to Dallas in 2016. Seven players each scored double-digit points, which set a record for a WNBA playoff game. Although the Wings lost to the Las Vegas Aces in the semifinals, Wings coach Latricia Trammell was pleased with her team's performance. At the postgame press conference, she said, "In the preseason they were not even supposed to make the playoffs . . . I'm just extremely proud of them."

A Big Win for the Wings

Latricia Trammell coached the Dallas Wings for two seasons, 2023 and 2024.

Chapter TWO

DALLAS WINGS HISTORY

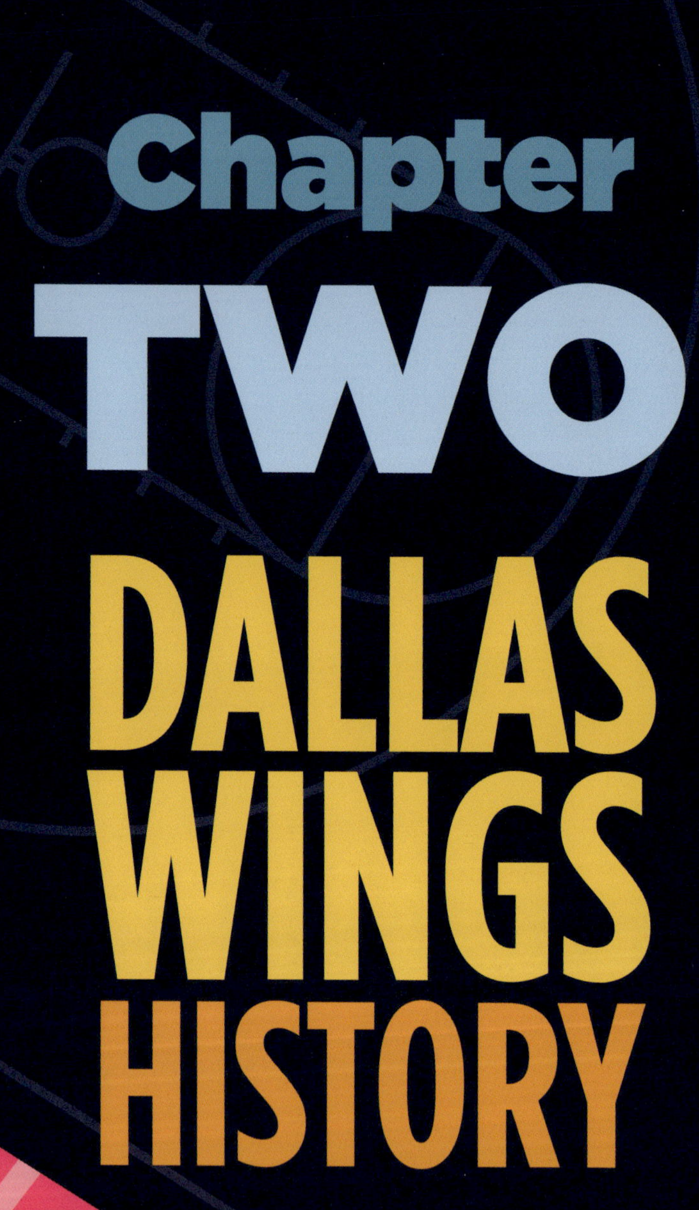

The team now known as the Dallas Wings began as the Detroit Shock in 1998. The Michigan team started well, even making the semifinals in 1999. However, by 2002, the Shock ranked last in the **Eastern Conference**. The owners even considered **disbanding** the team, but a new coach named Bill Laimbeer believed he could turn the team around.

CHAPTER TWO

He succeeded. In 2003, Detroit lived up to its name and shocked everyone when the team qualified for the playoffs, and later won the WNBA Championship. Detroit won the title two more times, in 2006 and 2008.

But 2009 brought hard times for the Detroit Shock. The city of Detroit was struggling **economically**. Few basketball fans could afford tickets to the games. The team was sold, and the buyers were from Tulsa, Oklahoma. This led the Detroit Shock to become the Tulsa Shock. The team also lost some of its best players, so during its Tulsa era, the Shock only qualified for the playoffs once, in 2015. That year, the Shock made it to the semifinals under a new coach named Fred Williams.

Detroit Shock center Kara Braxton during a 2006 game against the Connecticut Sun

FAST FACT

People often refer to the Shock as "the team that went from worst to first."

CHAPTER TWO

In 2016, team owner Bill Cameron announced he was moving the Shock to Arlington, a suburb of the Dallas-Fort Worth area. Cameron hoped this area's larger population would draw more people to the games. In a statement to the news, Cameron said, "We are thrilled to join [the Dallas-Fort Worth area], with a fan base that has a genuine love for their professional sports teams." The team was renamed the Dallas Wings.

The Wings now play at College Park Center on the University of Texas campus. Their new fans love to watch them play. Best of all, they have been in the WNBA Playoffs five times since the move.

Dallas Wings History

Dallas Wings forward Plenette Pierson during a 2016 game against the Chicago Sky

Chapter THREE

TEAM LEADERS

Coach Bill Laimbeer

Three coaches have led the team to big turnarounds, including Bill Laimbeer, Fred Williams, and Latricia Trammell. Laimbeer coached the team from 2002 to 2009. His **aggressive** coaching style helped the team win championship titles in 2003, 2006, and 2008. It also earned him the 2003 WNBA Coach of the Year award.

Williams coached the team from 2014 to 2015. With previous WNBA experience coaching the Utah Starzz and the Atlanta Dream, he led them to the semifinals in 2015. Williams continued coaching the team after the move to Dallas. Under his leadership, the Wings qualified for the playoffs in 2017 and 2018.

Trammell began her coaching career with record-breaking seasons at both the high school and college levels. In 2014 and 2015, her Oklahoma City University team became the **National Association of Intercollegiate Athletics (NAIA)** champions. She was named Coach of the Year for both seasons.

FAST FACT

The team's first coach was Nancy Lieberman. She led the team for its first three seasons when it was known as the Detroit Shock.

CHAPTER THREE

In 2017, Trammell started her WNBA coaching era as an assistant coach for the San Antonio Stars. She later served in the same role for the Los Angeles Sparks. Her successful coaching helped four Sparks players earn WNBA **all-defensive honors**.

In 2023, Trammell began her job as head coach for the Dallas Wings and led them to the semifinals for the first time since 2015. In 2024, the team had many injuries which prevented them from making the playoffs. Shortly after the end of the season, Trammell was replaced by Chris Koclanes. But Trammell's players always appreciated her supportive attitude. Arike Ogunbowale spoke about Trammell in a 2023 interview with *The New York Times*. She said, "You can just tell that she believes in every single one of us."

Team Leaders

Dallas Wings guard Arike Ogunbowale in a 2024 game against the Los Angeles Sparks

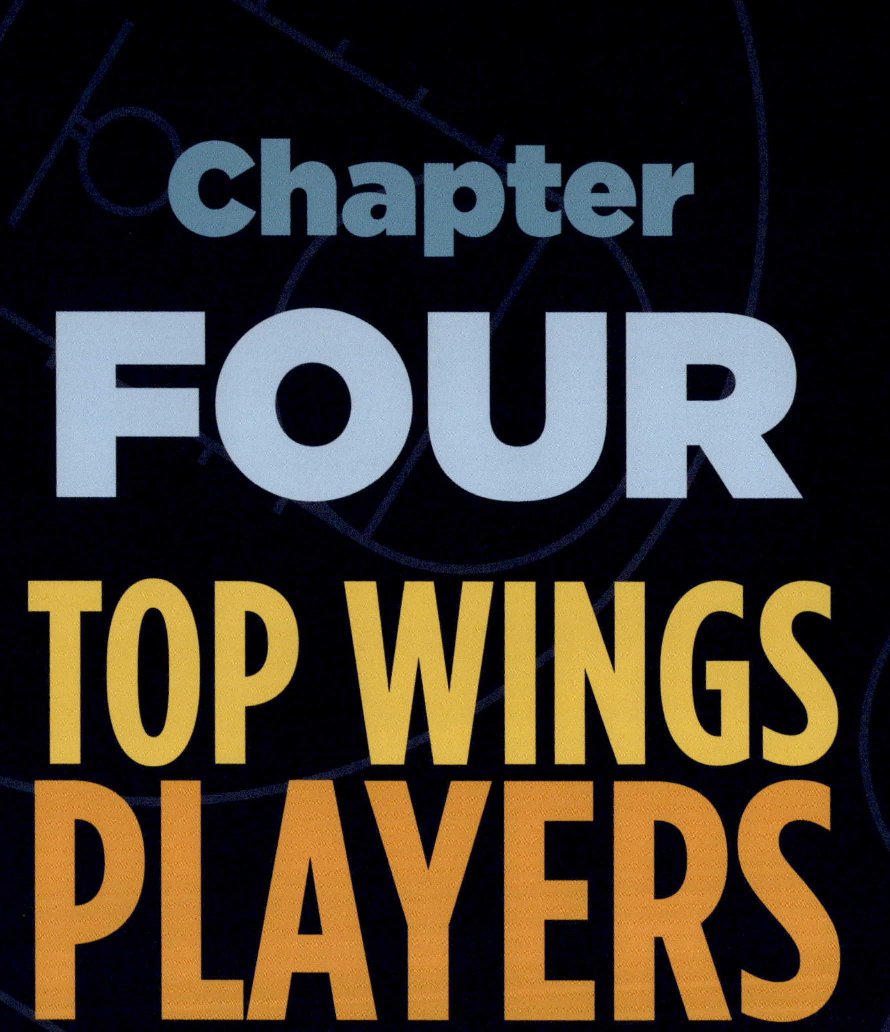

Chapter FOUR

TOP WINGS PLAYERS

Arike Ogunbowale

The Wings have many fantastic players. As a college student, Arike Ogunbowale had played for the University of Notre Dame. In 2018, she made a famous buzzer-beater shot that won the NCAA Semifinals game against the University of Connecticut in overtime. She later nailed a difficult three-pointer at the end of a national championship game, winning the title for Notre Dame. Her performance earned her the 2018 Female Athlete of the Year award.

CHAPTER FOUR

Ogunbowale joined the Wings in 2019. She averages more than 20 points per game as a Wings **guard**. She also matched a WNBA record for three-pointers during a Wings game against the Indiana Fever on September 1, 2024. Ogunbowale was the WNBA All-Star Game's Most Valuable Player (MVP) in both 2021 and 2024.

Satou Sabally was born in the United States in 1998. Her family moved to Gambia when she was two years old, and then to Germany for her school years. Sabally returned to the United States for college. During this time, she played for the University of Oregon. While there, she received the **PAC-12 Conference** Freshman of the Year award.

FAST FACT

During the 2024 All-Star Game against the U.S. Olympic team, Arike Ogunbowale scored 34 points, with a record-breaking 21 of them in the third quarter.

CHAPTER FOUR

Sabally left college early to play for the Wings in 2020. At 6-feet, 4-inches (1.9-m) tall, the powerful **forward** became a standout player. During a 2023 game against the Washington Mystics, she earned the Wings' first **triple-double** since the team's move to Texas. She played on the WNBA All-Star team in 2021 and 2023 and played for the German Olympic team in 2024 despite a shoulder surgery.

Dallas Wings fans enjoy watching their team play in person. In 2024, the team's season tickets sold out. In an interview with Fox 4 News Dallas-Fort Worth, WNBA reporter Dorothy Gentry said, "I think it's just part of the growth that we're seeing [in WNBA basketball]". The Dallas Wings hope to remain a part of this increasing excitement.

Top Wings Players

Dallas Wings forward Satou Sabally in a 2023 game against the Phoenix Mercury

GLOSSARY

aggressive
Coaching or playing in a way to dominate

all-defensive honors
The distinction of being named one of the five players of the WNBA's annual All-Defensive Team

disbanding
Breaking up a team so it no longer exists

Eastern Conference
The group of WNBA teams located in the eastern part of the United States

economically
Relating to the financial well-being of an area based on the buying and selling of goods and services

fast break layup
A basketball play in which a player makes a close-range shot before the opposing team can defend against it

forward
A basketball player who plays near the basket, often rebounding and scoring points

guard
A basketball player who focuses on passing, dribbling, and setting up plays

National Association of Intercollegiate Athletics (NAIA)
An athletic association for colleges and universities in North America

PAC-12 Conference
A group of college athletic teams located in the Western United States

triple-double
The achievement of double-digit scores in three categories during a single basketball game

SLAM DUNK WNBA TRIVIA

- At age nine, Satou Sabally was the only girl on her youth basketball team in Germany.
- Lightning is the Dallas Wings' mascot. She is a winged horse, a creature that the Dallas-Fort Worth area has used as a symbol for decades.
- Wings forward Natasha Howard plays in Turkey during the WNBA's offseason.
- Wings guard Lou Lopez Sénéchal plays in the Czech Republic during the WNBA offseason.
- Arike Ogunbowale competed on the ABC television show *Dancing with the Stars* in 2018.
- Kalani Brown and Teaira McCowan have been friends since childhood.

FIND OUT MORE

IN PRINT

Coffelt, Nancy. *Atlanta Dream*. Mitchell Lane Publishers, 2026.

Davidson, B. Keith. *WNBA*. Crabtree Publishing, 2022.

Matt Chandler. *Basketball's Best Coaches*. Capstone Press. 2024.

ON THE INTERNET

Dallas Wings.
https://wings.wnba.com.

"Dallas Wings," *ESPN*, n.d.
www.espn.com/wnba/team/_/name/dal/dallas-wings.

"Dallas Wings," *FOX Sports*, n.d.
www.foxsports.com/wnba/dallas-wings-team.

INDEX

About the Author

Jenny Crooks-Johnson is a children's author from Colorado. She and her family enjoy filling out their brackets each year and watching basketball games together. She would like to thank her basketball-loving friend Deanna Buck for her help with this book.